Herbal Cosmetics

Recipes for Hair, Face and Body Preparations
You Can Make from
Your Garden and Kitchen

Jim Long

Long Creek Herbs
Route 4, Box 730
Oak Grove, Arkansas 72660

Published by
Long Creek Herbs
Route 4, Box 730
Oak Grove, Arkansas 72660

Printed in the United States by Paul's Printing

ISBN #1-889791-02-4

Introduction

In 1 A.D., the Roman writer, Crito, published four books on cosmetic making. In just one of those books is found recipes for preserving and increasing hair growth, dyes for gray hair, bleaches and tints for hair, hair greases, tips for how to avoid wrinkles and keep skin clear. He also wrote about how to make eyebrow pencils, how to care for the nails, as well as directions for making mouthwashes, perspiration ointments and perfumes for the body.

Galen, another scholar generations later, wrote even more about personal beauty as part of his studies in the human sciences. Galen is credited with inventing the very first cold cream!

I have put together these mixtures and recipes for body preparations from readily-found materials. Many of the ingredients you can grow in your own garden; others are available in health foods stores, from herbal dealers or the local grocery store.

The instructions are meant to be informative, simple and useful, as I believe that the more enjoyable the process, the more likely you are to use the products.

With a written history of body preparations going back to 1, A.D., we have a wealth of herbal material to draw upon and a tradition that covers much of written history. These recipes and blends are meant for your use and enjoyment and I hope you will use them, experimenting and changing them to come up with recipes and methods of your own.

The Bath

Most of us dash to the shower, hurry to get ourselves ready for the day, rush out the door and into the hectic schedules of our daily lives. Seldom do we stop and enjoy the healthful, invigorating luxury of a real bath. Yet it is so simple to take a little bit of extra time to soak away the cares of the day. The bath is a perfect time to meditate, letting the mind and body rest. What better way to be good to yourself than to treat yourself to a soothing, soaking herbal bath at the end of the day?

Several recipes follow that will add to the pleasures of bathing. Make bath time a special time of the day, or if not a daily special bath, then reserve one time just for yourself each week.

Choose a time that you can be alone. Turn off the phone, lock the door, put on some soothing music and draw your bath water. Prepare a special drink, with or without alcohol, according to your preference.

"Special up" the room with candles and fragrances and reward yourself for your hard work and dedication to those around you. After all, if you don't take care of yourself first, you will not be able to take care of others!

The Famous
Magic-Waters Beauty Bath

Ninan de L'Enclos, a lady of eighteenth century France was widely known for her beauty. She reportedly kept her breath-takingly good looks well into her 70s and attributed her appearance to her daily magic waters beauty bath. Here is Ninan's recipe:

1/2 cup lavender flowers
1/2 cup chopped comfrey root
1/2 cup thyme
1/2 cup rosemary
(all ingredients are dry, but fresh can be used)

Pour a quart of boiling water over the herbs and steep for 20 minutes. Strain and pour liquid into the bath, or sponge on.

The lavender helps reduce puffiness, comfrey root is an emollient and rejuvenating, especially to aging skin. Thyme is a mild deodorant as well as antiseptic and rosemary is energizing and astringent. Rose petals or other flowers for fragarnce can be added, as well.

Bath Herbs

Consider pampering yourself with a luxurious bath. Warm the room, pour yourself a favorite cup of tea or other refreshing, relaxing drink and start filling the tub. Use 1/2 cup of bath herb blend from any of the following recipes. Tie the bath blend in a washcloth, held together with a rubber band, or put the herb mix in a cotton drawstring bag (available from the sources listed in the back of this book).

Put the bagged herbs in a pan of boiling water (about 4 cups of water) and turn off the heat under the pan. Let the herbs steep as the tub fills. Pour the bath "tea" along with the bag of herbs into the tub (make sure the bag or cloth of herbs remains closed so you don't have leaves floating around in your bath).

Immerse yourself in a delightful herbal bath, soaking your cares away. Afterward, wring out the herb-filled cloth, hang it up to dry and use the herbs a second time if you wish.

Herbs that are pleasant in the bath:

Almond.................... Powdered almonds are used as a mild abrasive in facial and body scrubs.

Basil....................... Relaxing addition to bath or steam.

Calendula................ One of the best herbs for the skin; healing for dry skin and problem skin conditions.

Chamomile.............. Good for oily skin, soothing sore muscles, reducing swelling, stimulating for the skin. Excellent hair rinse and lightener for light hair.

Chervil.................... Revitalizing.

Eucalyptus.............. Stimulating, opens sinuses, eases soreness.

Juniper Berries......... Astringent, antiseptic; used in bath and steams.

Lavender................. Rejuvenating, relaxing, fragrant.

Lemon Balm............ Rejuvenating, relaxing, fragrant.

Linden (Basswood).. Flowers excellent subtle fragrance and skin smoothing qualities.

Mint....................... Calming of nerves; sore-muscle relaxer and skin stimulant.

Marjoram................ Stimulating, invigorating, eases soreness.

Nettles................... Soothing and strengthening. Makes excellent hair rinse, particularly useful on damaged hair.

Oat Straw............... Mildly soothing, strengthening in bath.

Parsley................... Soothes insect bites, helps heal blemishes.

Peppermint............. Revitalizing skin stimulant, opens pores and sinuses.

Pine Needles........... Refreshing, soothing, healing for oily skin.

Roses...................... Fragrant, astringent, cleansing.

Rosemary................ Relaxing, rejuvenating, refreshing astringent. Excellent as hair rinse ingredient for darker hair types; used with sage on graying hair.

Sage....................... Soothes abrasions, astringent, fragrant.

Shavegrass.............. Especially good for troubled skin; combats skin and nail fungus.

Strawberry leaves... Cleansing, mildly astringent
Thyme..................... Muscle relaxer, antiseptic
Orange Blossoms...... Fragrant, relaxing
Peach Leaves.......... Skin softener
Wood Moss.............. Skin softener
Winter Savory........ Revitalizing

To make an herbal blend, choose from the list above. Pick herbs that combine for the purpose you have in mind. Here's a recipe for a relaxing bath using dry herbs:

Relaxing Herbal Bath

1 cup Peach Leaves
1/2 cup Roses
1/2 cup Lavender
1/2 cup Rosemary
1/2 cup Calendula Flowers
1/4 cup Nettles
1/4 cup Sage leaves
1/2 cup Epsom Salts
1/2 cup Borax

To use: Place 1/2 to 1 cup of the blend in a muslin drawstring bag or tie in washcloth. Pour 4 cups of boiling water over and allow the blend to steep while you are filling the tub. Pour the bath"tea" and the herbs in the cloth, into the tub.

Mix all together, adding a few drops of rose or lavender oil for fragrance if desired. Blend should be kept in an air-tight plastic bag or container, away from sunlight, for a day or so before using.

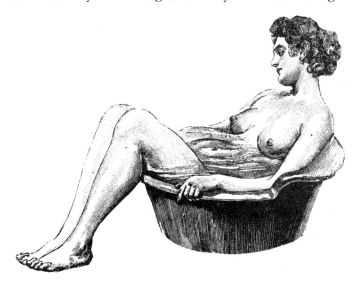

A Stimulating Bath Blend
to Wake Up the Skin and Muscles

1 cup Marjoram
1 cup Rosemary
1/2 cup Peppermint
1/4 cup Thyme
1/4 cup Juniper Berries
1/2 cup Borax
Optional:
8-10 drops Mint oil
8-10 drops Thyme oil

Luxury Bath
Choose this one to use on days you set aside to be really good to yourself.

1 1/2 cups Roses
1 cup Lavender
1 cup Calendula flowers
1 cup Shavegrass
1 cup Rosemary
1/2 cup Thyme
1/4 cup Mint
1 cup Wood Moss
2 cups Peach Leaves
10 drops Rose Oil
1 cup Borax
2 cups Epsom Salts

Mix and store until ready to use. To use, tie up 1/2 cup or more in cloth and steep in hot water while bath fills. Store in covered container, out of direct light.

6

Opens Your Head
and
Soothes Your Body Bath

2 cups Rosemary
1 cup Lavender
1 cup Eucalyptus leaves
1 cup Peppermint
1 cup Comfrey leaf
1 cup Thyme
1/2 cup Tarragon
1 cup Pine needles, chopped
2 cups Baking Soda
6 drops Lavender Oil
4 drops Eucalyptus Oil

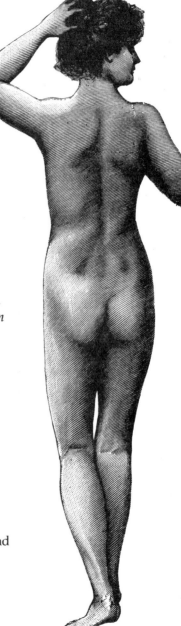

Troubled Skin Bath
for damaged or itchy skin
2 cups Shavegrass
2 cups Parsley
1 cup Rosemary
1 cup Thyme
1 cup Sage
2 cups Calendula flowers
1 cup Comfrey
2 cups Chamomile
1 cup Basil
2 cups Pine Needles
2 cups Nettles
3 cups Baking Soda

Use as a body/bath soak, and also as a face soak. To make a smaller amount, substitute tablespoons for the cups listed above.

7

Are You Going to Scarboro Fair Bath Blend

Recipe is given in "parts" which can be tablespoons, cups or pounds, depending upon how much you choose to make.

3 parts Parsley
3 parts Sage
3 parts Rosemary
3 parts Thyme

Mix well. Use 1/2 cup of the mix for each bath. Cover with 1 quart of boiling water and steep 30 minutes. Pour liquid into the bath.

Bath Oils

Bath oils you buy are simply vegetable oil with fragrance or herbs added. You can easily make your own.

Pine Needle Bath Oil

1/4 cup vegetable glycerin
1/2 cup chopped fresh pine needles
1/4 cup light mineral oil
1 oz. vodka
green food color

Combine pine needles and glycerin and leave covered for one week in a glass or plastic container. Strain. Combine this mixture with equal amount of light mineral oil. Add 1 oz. vodka and 1 drop green food color. Bottle. Shake before each use. The pine needles give a pleasantly woodsy fragrance and pine is cleansing and healthful on the skin.

Rose Bath Oil

1 cup vegetable oil of your choice
1/2 cup roses, fresh or dry

Combine, put in lidded jar or bottle. Shake daily for 1 week. Strain. If more fragrance is desired, repeat process with more roses in the same oil. Strain and use as moisturizer in the bath, using about 2 teaspoons per bath. May also be used as moisturizer directly on skin, then rubbed off.

Calendula Oil
For dry, flaking skin problems

1 cup Calendula flowers (dried)
1 1/2 cups vegetable oil (peanut, avacado or half corn oil, half
sunflower)

Combine flowers and oil in lidded jar or bottle. Shake daily for 1
week, then set aside for another week, shaking only occasionally.
Strain if desired (not necessary, you can leave the flowers in the oil if
you wish). To use: pour out small amount in hand and massage into
problem areas several times daily. This is the same marigold oil,
called calendulated oil, that you will find in the pharmacy and that is
recommended for many kinds of dry skin problems.

Up to Your Ears in "Potpourri" Bath Oil
A pleasant moisturizer for your skin

1 cup fresh flower petals (rose, jasmine, orange blossom, lilacs,
lavender, or a combination of any of those)
1/4 cup vegetable oil (peanut, corn, canola, almond or a
combination of those)
1/2 cup vegetable glycerin

Cover flower petals with glycerin in a glass bowl, mixing slightly.
Cover bowl with plastic wrap and put aside for 1 week, shaking briefly
every day or so. (It is best to keep this in the pantry or cupboard, away
from direct light). Strain glycerin and discard flower petals. Add vegetable oil, along with a few drops of food oil color if desired. Bottle.
When ready to use, shake, then add a few drops directly to the hot
bath.

About coloring oils: Regular food coloring is water-based and will
not mix with oil. To color oils you will need an oil-based food color, listed in the section on sources in the back of this book.

Vegetable oils for the bath include red turkey oil (one of the best
for bath oils if you are making a lot), peanut, canola, almond, avacado,
corn, sunflower and many others. Use an oil that feels good when you rub
it between your thumb and finger. Try mixing lighter oil, such as canola,
with corn or peanut oil, for a nice blend.

Herbal Bath Oil

1 cup of Marjoram, Lavender, or
Rosemary, or a combination of those
1/4 cup vegetable oil
1/2 cup vegetable glycerin

Cover herbs with glycerin in a glass bowl,
then cover bowl with plastic wrap. Shake occasionally, keeping bowl in dark place for a week.
Drain glycerin and discard herbs. Add vegetable
oil, along with a few drops of food color if desired. Bottle. When ready to use, shake, then add a few drops to the
hot bath. Sweet marjoram and lavender make an especially pleasant
bath oil, as does lavender by itself.

Rose Water-Glycerin Bath Oil

3 oz. vegetable glycerin
1 1/2 oz. rose water
1 1/2 oz. light mineral oil
3 drops red food coloring

Combine all ingredients in bottle. Shake together. Use several
drops in hot bath.

Rose Water-Glycerin
Hand Lotion

My mother's favorite hand
lotion was equal amounts of rose
water and glycerin. The mixture has
to be shaken before each use. This is
great for dishpan hands or chapped
hands and face in winter and leaves
your hands soft and smelling
pleasantly of roses. (Rose water is
available at many pharmacies).

Spicy Bath Oil

2 sticks Cinnamon,
broken
20 whole Cloves,
broken
2 oz. Safflower oil
2 oz. light Mineral oil
2 drops each red &
yellow food color

Combine in bottle and
set aside for two weeks.
Strain and rebottle, or leave
spices in the bottle, adding
more safflower oil and light
mineral oil as the first is
used. Several drops in the bath leaves
your skin smooth and spicy.

Slightly Exotic Bath Oil

1 1/2 oz. light Mineral oil
3 oz. Safflower oil
1 drop Clove oil
1 drop Orange oil
2 whole Cloves
1 Orange peel twist

Put all of the ingredients
together in a bottle and set aside
for two weeks, shaking occasionally. To use: add several drops to
bath.

Milk Bath

Milk whitens the skin, making it feel smooth and soft. Cleopatra, Queen of Egypt, known and remembered for her radiant beauty, claimed that her herb and milk baths were responsible for much of her loveliness. Here are the methods for making a good milk bath, updated for modern kitchens.

Fragrant milk bath consists of powdered instant milk, fragrance and any additional ingredients you choose. (Note: not all powdered milk is instant). You might also add borax, baking soda or Epsom salts.

Here's an easy recipe that will make you feel more beautiful every time you use it:

Rose Milk Bath

2 cups instant powdered milk
1 cup Epsom salts
4-6 drops rose oil
4-8 drops red food color

Put ingredients in food processor and pulse-process for about 30 seconds. Store in air-tight container until ready to use.

To use: take a handful and scatter in the tub as the water is filling. Swish around with hand to dissolve and get ready for a fragrant and relaxing beauty bath.

Optional: Use lavender oil instead of rose. Process half of mixture with 3 or 4 drops of blue food color and the other half with red food color, then combine the two and mix by hand.

Milk Bath with Baking Soda

2 cups instant milk
1 cup baking soda
1 cup Epsom salts
4-5 drops Rosemary oil
4-5 drops Thyme oil
Food coloring as desired

Follow directions for Rose Milk Bath

Milk Bath with Fragrant Herbs

2 cups instant milk powder
1 cup Epsom salts
1/2 cup borax
1/2 cup Marjoram
1/2 cup Lavender flowers
5 drops Lavender oil
Food color, optional

Process all ingredients in food processor in small batches.

To use: place about 1/2 cup or more in cloth bag or muslin drawstring bag. Drop in tub as it fills with water.

Almond Milk Bath

2 cups instant milk powder
1 cup baking soda
1 cup Epsom salts
5-6 drops Almond extract
4-5 drops yellow food color, optional

Process well in food processor.
Keep in airtight container until ready for use.

13

Bathing with Someone Special

While this isn't for everyone, some people like to share an occasional special bath with someone near and dear. To orchestrate this, consider making the place, the time, the ingredients, all very special.

Turn off the telephone, put the cat out, set aside the time when you won't be disturbed. Make the occasion as romantic, exotic and pleasurable as you like. Here are a few suggestions to consider:

Decorate the bath. Use lots of candles, fresh flowers, big fluffy towels. The room can be simple, but made to look inviting and exotic simply by using well thought out materials. Be careful if mixing the fragrances of candles with other things - use unscented candles and look to the bath oil and bath herb fragrances for the aroma of the moment. Too many scented things can take away from the mood you are trying to set.

Fix pleasant drinks ahead, possibly light, sensual snacks. Make up a bath blend and have it ready.

The mood is set, the bath is drawn, candles lit, now all you have left to do is entice that special person to get in the water with you.

Have drinks prepared ahead (in something other than a glass container; there's nothing worse, when the mood is romantic and you have to drain the tub to clean out broken glass!)

Have bath "tea" or bath oils prepared and ready for the tub in advance, also.

Include some light snacks. Here are a few suggestions:

Grapes - there's something **wonderfully romantic about two** people feeding each other grapes.

Brie - a good brie and some wine go a long way to get a mood going. Forget the **crackers; they get** soggy in wet hands.

Paté on bite-sized cucumber slices

Vegetable dip with carrot and celery sticks

Fruit, like sectioned oranges, peaches or other sensual fruit.

Olives. Lots of olives. Put one in your teeth and let your partner remove the pimento!

Beverages

For a relaxing bath alone, or to share a bath with someone special, mix one of the following drinks as a relaxing, refreshing beverage:

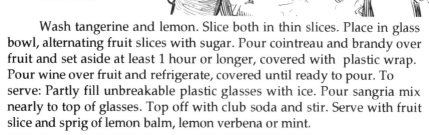

Sangria with the Bath

1 bottle Red Burgundy Wine
1 1/2 oz. Cointreau
2 oz. Brandy
1/2 cup Sugar
1 Tangerine
1 Lemon
Club Soda

Wash tangerine and lemon. Slice both in thin slices. Place in glass bowl, alternating fruit slices with sugar. Pour cointreau and brandy over fruit and set aside at least 1 hour or longer, covered with plastic wrap. Pour wine over fruit and refrigerate, covered until ready to pour. To serve: Partly fill unbreakable plastic glasses with ice. Pour sangria mix nearly to top of glasses. Top off with club soda and stir. Serve with fruit slice and sprig of lemon balm, lemon verbena or mint.

Non-Alcoholic Sangria

1 bottle Red Grape Juice or sparkling non-alcohol wine
3-4 drops orange extract
2 tablespoons fresh lemon balm, crushed
1/2 cup water
1/4 cup sugar
1 tangerine
1 lemon
1 can Sprite soda

Heat water in microwave to boiling. Add lemon balm and set aside. Slice lemon and tangerine, layering it in bowl with sugar. Add orange extract and refrigerate for 1-2 hours. Add red grape juice or sparkling wine along with lemon balm tea (strain first). Just before serving, fill glasses with ice, pour sangria nearly to top and fill glass with Sprite soda. Garnish with fresh lemon slice and sprig of lemon balm.

Shampoos

Fluffy Herbal Shampoo

Grate castile soap on kitchen grater to make:
    2 oz. (about 1/4 cup) castile soap shavings; add to:
    5 cups boiling water in which you have steeped 2 tablespoons each
    Lavender and Sage.

Pour boiling water over herbs and steep 2 hours. Strain and discard herbs. Bring water and soap shavings to almost boiling in the micro-wave. Stir to dissolve soap. When nearly cool, whip mixture with egg beater until fluffy. Scoop into wide-mouth jars or other containers. To use: dip fingers into shampoo and work into hair.

Oily Scalp Shampoo

5 cups herb water (follow directions above) made from:
1 cup dry chamomile flowers
2 oz. casatile soap shavings
3 oz. vodka or gin
Optional rose or lavender oil, adding
3 or 4 drops before whipping with
beater.

Mix soap and water over low heat in
pan, stirring until dissolved. Cool. Whip
with egg beather, beating in alcohol. Scoop into wide-mouth containers.

Hair Rinses

Herbal hair rinses are easy to make and pleasant to use. More like a strong herb tea, it rinses out soap residue, leaving your hair shiny, clean and smelling wonderfully herbal.

To use an herbal rinse:

Put the herb blends from any of the following recipes into 4 cups of boiling water (unless other amount is noted). Remove pan from heat, cover pan and set aside to let the herbs steep for 30 minutes. Strain and it is ready to use. After shampooing hair, pour herbal hair rinse through hair. You can catch and reuse liquid again if you choose. Rinse hair, or leave herbal rinse in hair.

Extra hair rinse will keep in the refrigerator for about 24 hours. To keep longer, up to a week, add 2 tsp. white vinegar. Heat amount desired in mircowave before pouring through hair.

Sage Rinse

5 tablespoons Sage leaves
1 quart boiling water
This leaves the hair clean and shiny, with the pleasant, herby fragrance of sage.

Sage-Rosemary Rinse
Especially good for dark or gray hair

4 tablespoons Sage leaves
4 tablespoons Rosemary leaves
1 quart boiling water

18

Lavender-Marjoram Rinse

1/4 cup Lavender flowers
1/4 cup Marjoram leaves

To use: put herbs into 3 cups boiling water. Remove from heat, cover and steep 15 minutes. Strain. Shampoo and rinse hair, then pour Lavender-Marjoram Rinse over hair. Leave in or rinse out.

Lemon Balm-Lavender Rinse

1/2 cup loosely-packed fresh Lemon Balm leaves
1/2 cup fresh or dry Lavender flowers
1/2 cup fresh Rose petals

Prepare as above, with 4 cups boiling water. Keep any unused portion in the refrigerator. If keeping longer than 24 hours, add 2 tsp. white vinegar and keep refrigerated.

Lavender-Oat Straw Rinse

1/2 cup chopped dry Oat Straw
1/4 cup Lavender flowers

Prepare as above, using 3 cups boiling water.

Damaged Hair Rinse

1 cup Nettles
4 cups boiling water.

Add Nettles to boiling water, remove from heat, cover pan and let steep while you shampoo and rinse hair. Pour Nettles Rinse over hair, catching excess and pouring over again. Don't rinse out. Wrap hair in towel and then dry hair as usual.

Faces

Sage Facial
Use 1/4 cup sage leaves (or
1/2 cup fresh)
2 cups boiling water
Bring water to boil, add
leaves and remove pan from
heat. Let steep for 10 minutes.

Lotion for
Legs or Face
Use like after-shave or body rub

2 oz. witch hazel
2 oz. gin
1 tsp. glycerin
Peel of 1 lemon
2 tsp. fresh or dry marjoram leaves

Combine all ingredients and set aside for 1 week, shaking every
day or so. Strain, or leave herbs in. Ready to use as after-shave or body
splash. You can also use fresh mint, lavender, sage or thyme in place of
marjoram.

Face Toner Wash
(as a steam or hot wash)
Ingredients can be fresh or dry:
1/4 cup Thyme (astringent and pore opener)
1/4 cup Mint (astringent, refreshener)
1/4 cup Sage (astringent, stimulant)

Pour 1 quart boiling water over herbs and
let steep for 30 minutes. Strain and reheat.
Soak face cloth in hot liquid and place on
face. Alternative method: bring to a steamy boil, remove from stove.
Cover head with towel, draping it over and around pan so as to allow the
steam to drift up around face. Use a mild, soothing oil or moisturizer
afterward.

Herbs that are also useful for
Lotions, Body-Splashes & After-Shaves:

Aloe........................Gel from Aloe Vera plant. Has drying effect on skin, removes oils, tightens skin.

Alum Root.............. Styptic properties

Calendula............... One of the very best herbs for dry skin.

Chamomile............. Good for oily skin conditions.

Citris...................... (Including orange, lemon, tangerine, etc.) - Strong astringent; peels used for milder astringency and fragrance. Use in water or witch hazel rather than directly on skin.

Comfrey leaves....... Excellent healing properties.

Juniper Berries .... Astringent, antiseptic, cleansing; use in body splashes and after-shaves.

Marjoram................. Stimulating, fragrant.

Mint........................Good in lotions and body splashes, as well as in the bath, due to the stimulating effects.

Peach leaves............ Skin softener and smoother.

Pine needles............. Refreshing and soothing for oily, troubled skin.

Rosemary................. Rejuvenating, refreshing and astringent.

Strawberry leaves... Cleansing, mildly astringent. Use as face wash, from a tea made from green or dried leaves.

Strawberries, fruit... Cleansing, astringent. Mash up berries and use as facial. Rinse and pat dry.

Thyme.................... Aromatic, antiseptic and disinfectant. Used as bath ingredient, as well as facial soak.

Winter Savory........ Revitalizing; used in facials, baths, lotions, after-shaves.

To make an herbal face soak:
Bring 2 cups of water to a boil. Turn off heat and add 1/4 cup dried herb of choice. Cover pan and let the herb steep for 10 minutes. Strain and use by soaking a face cloth and applying warm to the face. Leave cloth in place for 5 minutes. Repeat as desired. Facial tea can be reheated in the microwave, then discarded after use.

Herbs to Use for Fragrance:

Allspice..............pleasant, spicy fragrance, often used in combination with cloves and orange

Chamomile..........pleasant, clean fragrance. Used as a facial, chamomile flowers remove excess skin oils.

Citris peel............ astringent, fresh fragrance

Cloves.................. spicy fragrance

Eucalyptus............ stimulating on the skin, opens the sinuses

Lavender.............. rejuvenating, relaxing, fragrant. Excellent in the bath, in body powders, body splashes.

Mint..................... sinus opener, skin stimulant, fresh scent.

Roses................... astringent, cleansing, fragrant. Be sure the roses have not been sprayed with chemicals which may irritate your skin. Old varieties of roses can be grown without chemicals and many of those varieties have the best fragrances.

Other additives useful in body preparations:

Baking Soda......... softens water, helps reduce sting of rash, sunburn, scrapes and tired skin. Use with cornstarch for a refreshing dusting powder. Add fragrance or powdered herbs if desired.

Borax.................... adds light suds to bath blends; helpful mild soaking agent for the skin.

Calendulated oil... used for dry skin conditions, problem skin. The active part is calendula, an easily-grown flower, that can be combined in oil or aloe vera gel.

Cornstarch............ a purfied starchy flour made from corn that is the base of most body, baby and face powders.

Epsom Salts.......... magnesium; one of the best soaking agents for sore muscles or damaged skin.

Fuller's Earth....... highly absorbent clay used predominantly in talcum powders.

French Clay.......... finely ground absorbent clay used for facial mud masks. Works by drawing out the oils and returning trace nutrients.

22

A Useful Foot Bath:

Here's a recipe I concocted some years back to combat a tenacious case of athlete's feet. I had visited the dermatalogist several times over the years, getting perscriptions for medications that slowed the athlete's feet fungus but never stopping its return.

I knew that the herb Shavegrass (also called scouring rush and horsetail, the correct botanical name is *Equisetum hyemale*) is a good, natural fungicide for roses. Strong tea made from shavegrass, used as a spray, combats black spot and mildew on tea roses successfully.

So, I decided to try this natural fungicide on my feet. I made up a batch and soaked my foot every day for a week.

Not only did the foot soak stop the athlete's feet problem, the problem has not returned in the past 8 years! Here's my recipe:

    4 cups cider vinegar
    1/2 cup Shavegrass

Bring vinegar to a boil. Add chopped Shavegrass (fresh or dried). Continue boiling for 5 minutes, remove drom heat and cover pan with lid. Let this mixture steep overnight. Strain and discard herb. Pour the liquid into a plastic shoe box and cover with lid.

To use: keep the shoe box next to the shower. Every day after your shower, step into the shoe box of liquid and soak your foot for 2-3 minutes and pat dry. Repeat with other foot.

Lots of people have written back to tell me what a great job this recipe does in stopping fingernail and toenail fungus (the kind that causes the nail to turn black and eventually fall off). Most say that within 10 days the nail starts to grow back.

If you do not have access to the herb, Shavegrass, it is available by mail from Long Creek Herbs, Rt. 4, Box 730, Oak Grove, AR 72660.

Sources

Bulk herbs, "Make Your Own" cosmetic products kits for hair rinses & bath oils, bath blends, drawstring muslin bags, books and other products ($2 for catalog, refundable with order):
>Long Creek Herbs
>Route 4, Box 730
>Oak Grove, AR 72660
>(417) 779-5450; FAX: (417) 779-5450
>*Wholesale inquiries welcome*

Bulk dried herbs, seeds, plants, books, hard to find supplies ($2 for catalog, refundable with order):
>The Rosemary House
>120 South Market St.
>Mechanicsburg, PA 17055

Decorative bottles (in any quantity), food coloring for oils, glycerin, cosmetic oils, powder bases (catalog $3):
>Lavender Lane
>5321 Elkhorn Blvd.
>Sacramento, CA 95842
>(916) 334-4400; FAX: (916) 339-0842

Rose Hand Lotion

Equal parts Rosewater and glycerin. Shake before each use. Leaves hands smooth and pleasantly fragrant.

Scar Lotion for Stretch Marks

2 parts camphorated oil
3 parts peanut oil
3 parts dissolved lanolin

Mix well & put in small container. Massage areas several times daily.

Skin Wash for Problem Skin

1/4 oz. Slippery Elm
1 oz. Echinacea root
2 oz. Burdock root
1 3/4 oz. Strawberry leaves
1/4 oz. Witch Hazel herb
1/4 oz. Chamomile flowers
3-4 drops Orange oil
2-3 drops Cinnamon oil

Mix. To make wash, bring 1 1/2 cup of water to boil. Add 2 Tbsp. of herb mix. Remove pan from heat, cover with lid and let steep for 15 minutes. Wash face first with mild soap and water, then wash with herbal liquid. Repeat 3 times daily.

Chamomile Face Soak
(for oily skin)
4 Tbsp. Chamomile flowers
2 cups water

Bring water to boil and add Chamomile flowers. Turn off heat and cover pan with lid. Let steep 15 minutes. Strain.
Reheat liquid in microwave so that it is slightly hot. Soak washcloth in the warm liquid and lay washcloth over face. Leave on until washcloth begins to cool, then repeat process.

Sitz Bath for Bruises
(from Jerry Stamps)
1 cup comfrey leaves
1 cup Life Everlasting
1/2 cup Lemon Balm leaves
1/2 oz. Lobelia
1/2 oz. Rosemary

Mix. Steep a handful in 1 qt. boiling water for 20 minutes. Add liquid to stiz bath and soak at least 20 minutes daily.

Comfrey-Aloe Facial

4-5 small to medium sized fresh comfrey leaves
1 cup Aloe Vera gel

Put both ingredients in blender and blend to a smooth paste. Apply paste to face and smooth over. Let dry, about 7 minutes, then wash off.

Galen's Cold Cream, updated
(a 1st Century writer & physician)

1/2 cup almond oil
1/4 cup water
1 Tbs. beeswax
1 tsp. borax

Slowly heat ingredients in safe container in microwave. Remove from microwave and stir while liquid cools. To give a fragrance, use 1/4 cup infusion (tea) made from boiling water and 2 tsp. herbs of choice (such as roses, lavender, mint or rosemary).

Fingernail Hardener
(Jerry Stamps)
3 Tbsp. water
1 Tbsp. glycerin
1 tsp. powdered alum

Mix & paint on nails before bed time. Remove in the morning with rubbing alcohol.

Skin Toner
1/2 cucumber, peeled & seeded
3 Tbsp. fresh Mint leaves
1 Tbsp. Aloe Vera gel
5-6 drops vitamin E oil

Put ingredients in blender and blend until smooth, about 1 minute. Spread on face and massage in well. Leave on for 10 minutes then wash.

Mondarda Tea

1 Tbsp. Monarda flowers
2 cups boiling water

Pour boiling water over Monarda flowers. Cover and let steep for 5 minutes. Strain and sweeten with honey. Makes a refreshing drink in winter or summer.

Mint Mouthwash
2 cups vodka
1 cup water
2 cups mint, packed down

Put mint, vodka and water in glass or plastic container and secure lid. Keep in a place out of sunlight, such as in the kitchen cupboard or pantry. Shake contents daily. Ready to use in a week. To use: add a tablespoonful to a couple of ounces of water and rinse mouth after brushing.

Jerry's Massage Oil

4 oz. Almond oil
10 drops Orange oil
10 drops Lime oil
5 crops Cucumber oil
5 drops Vanilla oil
2 drops Cinnamon oil

Other books by Jim Long

Herbs, Just for Fun - How to Grow & Use Herbs

Just for Men - Body Preparations from the Garden for Men

Dream Pillows & Potions

Tea & Cakes Under the Trellis - How to Make Bentwood Trellises with Recipes for Tea & Cakes

How to Make Romantic Bentwood Garden Trellises, Arbors, Gates and Flower Border Fences

Classic Blends - The Seasoning Blends of the Ages

Recipes & Cooking Practices of the Civil War

Herbal Medicines of the Santa Fe Trail

How to Get Free Publicity for Your Business or Organization

Guide to Successful Self-Publishing

How to Plan and Host Successful, Profitable Festivals

If you would like information about our programs and workshops for your group or organization, request our Programs Brochure.

For a complete list of all of our books and herb products, send $2 (refundable with first order) to:
Long Creek Herbs
Route 4, Box 730
Oak Grove, Arkansas 72660

Wholesale inquiries welcome